RELIGIOUS EYE OPENER

RELIGIOUS EYE OPENER

Peter Knoester

TATE PUBLISHING
AND ENTERPRISES, LLC

Published by Tate Publishing & Enterprises, LLC
127 E. Trade Center Terrace | Mustang, Oklahoma 73064 USA
1.888.361.9473 | www.tatepublishing.com

Tate Publishing is committed to excellence in the publishing industry. The company reflects the philosophy established by the founders, based on Psalm 68:11,
"The Lord gave the word and great was the company of those who published it."

Cover design by Nino Carlo Suico
Interior design by Shieldon Alcasid

Published in the United States of America

ISBN: 978-1-68164-348-9
Religion / Christianity / General
15.07.02

CONTENTS

FOREWORD

There was an urge in me to write about some of my religious beliefs. I am by no means an expert on religion, but what I do know, I did write about. I am sure there will be people who will totally disagree with me, but that is only their opinion the same as I have mine. It all will be revealed one day as we all must cross the river Jordan as they say. There is no doubt what the reformers of old had in mind when they wrote about the Christian faith, what they thought about their reason for being where they were at that time. I am sure that the inspiration of the Holy Spirit was the main cause for them to write as well as preach the gospel to the people. There are people who disbelieve what is written in the Bible, and like many others, it is very hard to believe. The Bible is, however, a book that has been written by people who were also inspired by the Holy Spirit. It does not matter if some of the historical data are not overly accurate as long as the relationships with God are accurate as that is the spiritual message given for everyone to see and understand. I have come to realize that the Old Testament is mostly about God and the promise of the Son, while the

New Testament is mostly about the Son and the promise of eternal life. There is a God, and we are all his creation. We must adhere to what the Bible teaches us, like it or lump it. Anyway, my thoughts on a great many things, I put down on paper and I hope that many a person may see it the way I do or be enlightened by the words I wrote.

1

WHO AND WHAT IS GOD?

Why these questions arise in me, I don't really know. It seems that most people have the answers except me. I was thinking about who and what God is and what He is all about. I know one thing that the Godhead is not just one but Three in One called the Elohim, and there is no separation at any time. These three were from the beginning of time, and as a matter of fact, created time to have everything we see come into being. Anything from the smallest atom to the greatest star or heavenly body in the universe is their creation. Seeing and understanding of it all should make us stand in awe when we look at our own self and our so-called abilities. God is not some old man with a beard, and neither is the Son or the Holy Spirit; they are as they always were as a person in his or her strength say at about the age of thirty. All we see was created by the Son on command of the Father and is sustained by the Holy Spirit who instilled into everything the laws that governs it all. We may call it the laws of nature, anything from what holds the tiny atom together to magnetism, the laws of gravity and all the other forces that holds the universe together. Anything that has life is also governed by the laws instilled in it. We don't have to go far to see this in everything from the smallest of plants to the greatest of animals. These laws also govern us all and the functions of our bodies testify of this. The only part of us that is separate is our spirit, or soul if you will. It is subject to other forces that cannot be explained, except to say that evil forces can influence us to the extent that we will become a slave of whatever this evil force has intended for us to do.

It is stated here that a belief in an almighty entity is the only thing that prevents us from becoming indeed a slave of the evil one. We must have an understanding of our eternal nature, which is that part of us that gives us the desire to become one again with the Elohim where we were when the worlds were formed. Our soul was there, and there must be in us a longing to become one again with the Elohim. The journey after birth on this earth is like a battleground because of the so-called free will given us at the fall of Adam and Eve. We have so many desires in us to please this earthly body that we tend to forget the need of our spiritual being to be immortal in that part that we were in before we were born. Let us look at nature and see how everything is regulated by forces unknown to us, from plants to animals to the planets and stars and the universes yet to be discovered. We see that everything there is has an end and that nothing is or lasts forever except the Elohim. I will elaborate on the need of a religious belief given by our Creator and its purpose in our lives in another chapter.

2

THE WORLD

As I sit here and contemplate life, I come to realize how little we can hold and encompass. The eyes can only see so far, and the ears can hear only the things within range. And just the same, we think we are somebody. The world flies through space at tremendous speed, and the surface of the earth itself has a speed of over one thousand miles per hour. And here we stand, thinking we are somebody. The atrocities committed in the name of a king or ruler of a nation, tribe, or even a family are beyond understanding and seem to be rooted in a belief that as long as we ourselves are in safety, it is alright. What foolishness to think that we are somebody special. The empires of the past have all gone by the wayside, although in some cases there are remains of their existence to be found; nevertheless, they are gone, and all the sacrifices of these empires in the form of all the young men who fought for this or that ruler have been, in hindsight, in vain. Even now, the world is full of people who wish to form a religious empire to which all the world must adhere to or be put to death. All the lessons from the past don't mean anything, only the present is catered to.

When I see and hear about the extremists of the Islamic faith who will kill anyone not of their faith or belief, I see no middle ground and love for a fellow human being is totally absent. It is a totalitarian regime that governs the Islamic states. The car bombings—as well as the so-called suicide bombers that kill countless people, which is also of the Islamic faith—is totally beyond comprehension. I realize that it is mostly to destabilize a government that does not totally adhere to teachings of the Koran. When we see the Western worlds so-called being overrun by people of the Islamic faith whose leaders openly state that these nations will eventually become Islamic, is not far away from the truth. Schools in some cities in Europe have now an over 50 percent student population from Islamic parents. The main reason for this is that a man of the Islamic faith can have three or more wives and thus produces more children than couples that marry only one spouse. It does not take a mathematician to calculate the far-reaching consequences of this one-sided problem.

Is there a solution to this problem? I wonder. Would the ban of polygamy or adaptation of China's one-child policy in the Western world help solve this problem? As a young boy, I saw the people of the Jewish faith taken from their homes and put into trucks and transported to so-called concentration camps, only to be exterminated. It is my hope that this will not happen in our day and age to the people of the Islamic faith—to also get taken from their homes and send back to the countries they came from if the rage of the Western worlds ignites because of the atrocities committed by the extremists claiming to be of the Islamic faith—especially after 9/11, which is likely only the start of our sorrows. There is no end to the cruelties committed by nations in power over the past two thousand years. In our day and age, with the density of the population, a lot more people will be affected. One does not have to go very far back when the atomic bomb used during the Second World War was used to expedite the end of the war, how tens of thousands were killed in a few seconds and thousands more died of their injuries. I believe us to be on the very edge of a war of a proportion that we have never seen before in which millions upon millions will die because of weaponry used that will wipe out whole populations in a matter of minutes. It is very likely that the state of Israel will be in the middle of this conflict between the Islamic forces as well as the forces from Russia and China. There is no doubt in my mind that there will be atomic warfare as we have never seen before, and this will be the end of an age and the beginning of another perhaps the Age of Aquarius.

3

THE COMING STORM

The time that the Islamic states will try to raise their flag over countries that have a large Islamic population is close at hand. The atrocities committed by the Islamic extremists passes even the atrocities committed by the German Nazis during the Second World War. The murderous hordes of the Middle East have no mercy for any fellow human being, or even their fellow Muslim who is not totally dedicated to the will of Allah and his teachings. The time will shortly come to pass that the "free" nations of the Western world will be subjected to the demands uttered by the people of the Islamic faith that live in those countries. Let no one be mistaken about this as there will be bloodshed in the streets, and most governments will have no choice but to round up all those of the Islamic faith and put them into concentration camps awaiting the deportation to the countries they came from. When Japan declared war on the United States, the citizen of Japanese nationality were all rounded up and put into concentration camps to safeguard the nation from bloodshed within. We all know what happened to the people of the Jewish denomination during the Second World War. They were done away with as nothing ever stopped Nazis and were systematically murdered by a race that was always of the highest and most intellectual of the Western world—a race that brought forth the great composers, the greatest of painters and most of all, the reformers of the Christian faith. You may ask, what happened over there? How was it possible for all this to come about? We all know, with a few exceptions, that the German people themselves were responsible for the rising of that demonic government. Now, in this day and age, we see the same thing happening in other nation were the rule of law is thrown out of the window and only the law of Islam exists, which only purpose is to bring this belief to all the world and has started to do so already. We have seen to what extreme these people are willing to go, and the proof of this we saw on September 11 when all those people in the Twin Towers were sentenced to death. Even now, some businesses owned by Islamic people celebrate the martyrdom of the people who commandeered these planes and died for the cause on September 11. It may be too late to stop the onslaught of these events to come about, but something must be done to curb and to prepare for the coming violence that is just over the horizon. I may be called an alarmist and a worrier, but I am sure that a lot of people are in agreement with me and would like to see the Western world taking a stand against the people of these Islamic states by taking no more immigrants, isolation and sanctions of the dire kind, as well, and if needed, military actions.

4

MORE ABOUT ISLAM

There is no doubt in my mind as a Christian that Satan's army consists of people of the Islamic faith, of which the ISIS extremists are the foremost perpetrators of the atrocities committed against the people of the Christian faith and anyone who does not embrace Islam. The cruelties committed by these forces go beyond comprehension, and it becomes more obvious day by day that they operate indiscriminately even against their own people. They know not and do not conform to any democratic concept on which most of the Western societies are based. The existence of individual rights is totally alien to them as is the right to worship to a god or deity of the people's choosing. Love for a fellow human being who is not of the Islamic faith or compassion for them is also alien to them as the root of all evil prevents that, Islam has no place for that sort of thing. The promise to the suicide bombers of getting so many virgins and all the pleasures in the afterlife is all a delusion, as the afterlife is on a spiritual realm where everything earthly has been done away with as that is the sole reason for living well and to act in this life to the honor of God Almighty. Heaven is a place where all the saved souls sing praises to the Lamb and the Father of all human beings for they were saved from eternal death and live and love forever more until all eternity. The elation of that has no end and if you like, the "high" because of it, never ends. Nothing the earth had to offer will be in heaven as it would be, for a better word, "unclean." There will be no sports no entertainment, except worship, no games of any kind as all that is not needed anymore as the soul is full of the things heavenly and has no need of these things anymore. Our God will be center of all things, but the "center piece" in heaven will be the Son who is obedient to the father and accomplished all that was required of him. We are the product of his sacrifice. We will experience the presence of God but will not be able to see him; however, we will see the one who has given us eternal life, and He will be like a brother to us as we too will be called the children of the Most High through Jesus Christ our Lord, and amen to that.

5

ABOUT DEMONS

What can I say about demons as they seem to be everywhere, including in me at times. They are, in my opinion, forces in the world as well in the universe that are opposite to whatever there is that we know. Like life opposed to death or good and evil or substance versus antimatter. Demons have the ability to possess a being without this being knowing that he is possessed. From the beginning of time, there have been indications that even in the animal world, they are the peacefully grazing animals and the ferocious ones preying on them whether at the time of the dinosaurs or in the present time. When we go back in history, we see that the empires that followed one another were all led by people or a person who was in the control of a demon, or devil if you will. The likes of Attila the Hun or Alexander the Great, the kings of Babylon or the rulers of the Medo-Persian Empire, as well as in modern times the German kaiser or Hitler all were possessed with a demonic being and so were doing the will of this demonic being as it dictated.

To where all this is leading us is a mystery to me, but I can see that anyone committing an offense against another human being is in that category. We all live our lives as parents, or a guardian taught us or try anyway, but sometimes we will open the door for the evil one to come in and to destroy our lives if we let it. Sometimes the willpower to reject this force is absent or one is overcome and we could end up in a tragic situation from which is no escape. The very thought of disliking another human being can be the beginning or a start of a murderous thought brought about by a demonic power. When I see the people who possessed powers that go beyond normal abilities, then you can be sure that a demonic force is at work. I have seen things done by a magician that defy logic as well as by others who do things that are normally impossible to be done by a "normal" person. Perhaps a person may say what a pessimist I am, and they are probably right as I have a tendency to be like that. However, anyone who has seen what I have seen, these people do has to admit that what they do is virtually impossible. Because of this, I have come to see that in the end, there is no time, there is no present, and no future—it is all one. When we observe on the television or internet what the space telescope Hubbard let us see, we discover that, to quote David the king of Israel, "We are but a speck of dust on a weighing scale." It won't affect the weight of what is being weighed. In other words, although we are much more than the highest of mountains because we are alive, we still are very insignificant in the realm of things like the universe. Sometimes I think that all the world and all the people around me are there just for me, and the illusion of that makes me feel like an important part of the whole universe while leaving me like an helpless individual who is tossed to and fro in the ocean of life at the same time.

6

WHAT DOES IT MEAN TO BE BORN AGAIN?

In the Bible, Jesus told Nicodemus that unless a person be born again, that person could not enter the kingdom of heaven. Nicodemus was a teacher in the Jewish faith and thought he knew about the Torah etc., but he asked Jesus how can a grown man go back into the womb and so be born-again. Needless to say, this did not apply to the physical but to the spiritual. There are so many examples in the Bible that points to this state as it were, and some are very hard to understand, especially when Christ says that a person who does not leave anything behind including his family, friends, and neighbors, and even hates his own life "is not worthy of me." These may not be the exact words, but we understand where this leads us. We will be a separated entity whose own life is only to be lived for him who gave up his life for him or her.

The most instant born-again experience happened to the apostle Paul on his way to Damascus to imprison more people who believed in the Christian faith. We all know this story as told in the Bible and we all know what became of Paul. He became the greatest of all the apostles and became the greatest of teachers in the faith. To be born again is a state of being where no earthly goods, may it be possessions, riches, or anything earthly matters and only the desire to be with the one who died for them on the cross matters so that he could cleanse them from all their iniquities and give them as it were a free pass to heaven.

7

WHAT IS HEAVEN?

Heaven is a place where all the heavenly beings like the angels reside, where Christ is the center piece, and where God's presence is not seen but felt and known in a way that is indescribable. All the people who are in heaven by God's grace and the sacrifice of the Lamb will be clothed in white robes and have spiritual bodies. There won't be any babies there as they all will have become grown-ups the instant they passed away. There will not be any old people there either but all will be as they were in their strength, say around the age of thirty. There will be no memories of earth as all earthly thoughts will have disappeared as it were and only the praising of him who made it all possible will be heard. We will be in a constant state of elation, which will have no end. There will be no games, no computers, no sports—nothing that would remind us of earth will be there. Heaven would almost be like a person who has experienced weightlessness except a million times better.

There will be no need to eat; ergo, no toilets are needed. The understanding of everything, including creation itself, is seen as in God's eyes as we will be as sons and daughters of God and will have the same heart and mind as it were.

I believe that anyone, including myself who has had an out of body experience, will come close to that state of a heavenly being, all for now.

8

WHAT ABOUT WARS?

It is a subject that has been on my mind for a long time now. I was only about ten years old when the Second World War came to an end in Holland, but I saw things that had a lasting effect on me. I still remember all those years later. What is the reason behind wars, I asked myself. I came to the conclusion that they are caused by the greed of certain individuals who are in control of power through government. But before I go on, I must say that any conflict has an origin, which usually starts in the brain of someone. Take the Bible story of Cain and Abel for instance. Cain slew Abel because he thought that God liked his brother better than him. This was the first war in the history of the world even though only two people were involved.

When we go back through the centuries, we see that there were always people who wanted to build an empire for themselves either to be remembered perhaps or to become immortal in the ages to come. We all know about those empires that conquered so many other countries and exacted a toll not only in human lives but also in the paying of tributes. There is no doubt in my mind that evil forces were at work here as it took over the leader of a family, tribe, or nation who then, with demonic power, would be able to do as this force allowed him.

The presence of evil forces in this world of ours is not something that we are not aware of; one does not have to go very far or even look inward to discover this. When one sees two people yelling at one another at the top of their voice about something or another, we can see that hatred is in this and that evil has taken hold. When we go back a hundred years, at the start of World War I, we see how one man called a kaiser started this conflict under the pretense of an event that took place in Sarajevo in the form of an assassination. We saw how one man caused the death of so many countless millions of soldiers as well as civilians. We ask ourselves whose fault is this, and the answer lies in the fact that that person was taken over by a demon and so did that demon's bidding. Sure there are other factors that can be blamed for the tremendous loss of life, including the incompetence of generals still living in the glory days of old and were out of touch with modern warfare. After this war was over, a pact was made to prevent something like this to ever happen again. We all know that less than twenty-two years later, another demon-possessed entity came to power and started World War II. The terrible loss of lives, as well as the heinous crimes committed during this war, is a proof that evil indeed exists in the world. There is no doubt in my mind that the German soldiers of the so-called SS were demon possessed and acted accordingly, being totally without pity or concern about the people they killed, maimed, or tortured.

Now there is a new threat in the world, and it will come from the extremist Islamic forces, which will embroil this world once again in a conflict that will have dire consequences for all of us.

9

WAR AND ITS CONSEQUENCES

At times, when I watch the news or receive e-mails pertaining to past or ongoing conflicts and hear about the terrible toll in human life, I wonder where it will all end. It seems that evil forces will always be with us no matter how hard we try to prevent bloodshed in the name of an entity, nation, or religion. There are nations that have always carried the brunt of freeing the people who are conquered by another nation. Nations like the United States, England, Canada, Australia, and others who stand united in the fight against the enslavement of others. There seem to be no end to the parade of a Nebuchadnezzar, Genghis Khan, Alexander the Great, or like in the twentieth century a kaiser, Mussolini, a Hitler, a Hirohito, or a Stalin who thought they could conquer other nations and use their resources to enrich their own nation.

I have also come to realize that if it were not for the fallen soldiers during all these conflicts from the beginning of time, the world would be so overly populated that perhaps this world would go hungry because it would have billions of mouth to feed. This is just an afterthought of mine and does not take away any of the anguish and tears shed over loved ones who died for their king and country, whether they be friend or foe. When I hear and see in my mind's eye the sobs of the wives, mothers, as well as the children who lost a husband, son, or father, then I want to take them in my arms and lend them my shoulder to cry on to ease the pain within. Yes, they died for their country, but why did it come this far? Could it have been prevented via negotiations or making certain allowances? Who is to blame? The politicians, the producers of weaponry, which we all know is big business. The weapons factories seem to give out weaponry indiscriminately to individuals or any nation willing to pay for them. I realize that shutting them down would cause a severe depression as thousands upon thousands would be without a job, which in turn could cause social unrest with some dire consequences. We are as it were in a hopeless situation, and the conflicts will go on and on and so many more will be killed so senselessly as the love for money or lands overtakes all those who have no love for their fellow man. I have come to see that this world is becoming more and more violent. The children nowadays have computer games of very violent nature wherein killings are rampant. The incidents of violence in schools are increasing at a tremendous pace. Our children have lost respect for their elders. Many mothers are raising a child alone, as the divorce rates are skyrocketing, leaving the raising of the child to others who may not care as much for them as a mother or father would, as long as they get paid.

I really don't like to write about all this as it seems so negative as it were, even though a lot of this is true. The world seems to be in a sinkhole and only very few are aware of this, and when it all caves in, we all will become aware.

10

WHO IS THE RULER OF OUR WORLD?

Nobody will like what I am about to write, including myself but the truth must prevail. There is no doubt in my mind that the ruler of this world is Satan and his henchmen. He was with us in the garden of Eden and will remain with us until the end of time as we know it. His destruction on judgment day will be the end of him and his cronies, never to be seen again along with his followers who despised the saving grace of our Lord Jesus Christ.

Personally, I am a lover of sports and love to play chess as well as checkers. Cards is also one of my favorites past times. The game of ice hockey during the winter month also uses up quite a bit of my time as well as football etc. I am sure you have the picture by now. When I watch the games being played on the TV and I see the people in the stands cheer for "their" team, I have come to realize that this borders on idolatry. Did I mention movies as that, too, take up quite a bit of my time, hours on end? Reading, too, of the Western variety is a past time I enjoy. When I think back and realize the many hours that I spend on these entertainments, I see that as a, lets say, semireligious person, my soul that is on its way to eternity does not get the attention it needs to be ready for that event that my death will bring. The apostle Paul stated that anything that he has, like possessions, money, lands, etc., he considers to be dung compared to the knowledge of Jesus Christ our Lord.

Here is what I did not want to write about, namely, that all entertainment, sports, games, and yes even the world of electronics, are inventions of him who hates our Lord Jesus Christ who thought us the true way to heaven and how to spend our time on earth until his coming again, which will be quite soon when we see all the prophecies come about. I know that we cannot stop our thoughts from propping up in our heart and mind, and some are of the terrible kind and not fit to be known to others, but these thoughts cannot be avoided as we have so little control of them. The expression in the Bible "Pray without ceasing" is one expression that we all should adhere to as the tempter is always close by to take us into captivity if he could.

Sometimes I think what harm it could do if I watch sports if I live right, not realizing that I follow a golden idol that has no strength or staying power after the game is over. As with all games of any kind, it always will be "I am better than you." There always will be winners and losers with at times bitter feelings and hurt egos, which will give room for wrath or hard feelings, and then Satan rubs his hands in triumph as that is his goal in all games. Yes, there is sportsmanship, and a handshake will take place at times but those are far and wide in between. I see all these things in my mind's eye and hate myself for writing this down as almost all who read this will disagree with me and call me a party pooper, and rightly so as that is what I am and I am sorry to be like that; nevertheless, it is my opinion in view of religion.

11

A PRAYER

The word *prayer* props up quite often in a song or in poetry and of course is used in churches all over the world. To explain what it is and what it accomplishes is a subject that needs to be thought about deeply to explain this. I have come to realize that many of us at one time or another have send up a prayer to him who is all-knowing. There are a lot of people who have prayed a lot for one thing, not necessarily for themselves but for others who perhaps are ill or are in need of one thing or another. However, their prayers may not have been answered and they are wondering why that is. What the answer is, I don't really know. I only know that God is an entity who has supreme reign over everything—may it be an illness, material goods, or one's spiritual being.

There are a lot of examples in the King James Version of the Bible. According to the book of Psalms, David was still God's anointed despite displeasing him. Also, prayers were his way to communicate with him. We, too, are his creation and have the same needs that King David had. We have to come to him with openness and with a heart that is true and confess our sins to him and asked him to cleanse us from all our iniquities through Jesus Christ, his Son, before we ask for whatever is in our hearts. It is similar to a ritual that was performed by the high priest in the temple when he would sprinkle the blood of the slain lamb on the altar, which indicated that the sins of the people were forgiven for that year until the next time.

I know this is a deep subject, and we have to realize that life is in the blood and only blood could be used for the atonement of the sins of the people. This, of course, saw on the coming of the Christ and his atoning work for all the world by the shedding of his blood for those who were chosen before the worlds were formed. This, too, is a deep subject that is almost incomprehensible, but who am I to argue with God on this subject? He was from the beginning and will be there in the end of times, the Alpha and the Omega who is no respecter of persons and only take those of a pure heart regardless of their shortcomings. The mystery of life is in the fact that we are created in his image in the garden of Eden but have lost this image. And God wants it back the way it was then, before the evil one ruined it all. Fortunately, God had a fail-safe plan in his Son who was the only one who is able to bring about the reconciliation between God and men.

Prayer is the way. Although the road is sometimes rough, it is the only way to find access to the Father, just like David said, "Deep calls onto deep." When the lonely soul cries out to its maker to be reunited again with him for all eternity as it was in the very beginning of time when all the souls were still with God the Father.

12

THE REASON AND NEED FOR RELIGION

The question as to why we need religion has been on many a persons mind. From this stems all the controversies as to the whys and why nots. We all have an idea, and mine is that if there is a God, there must be a way to contact Him. So when we embrace a religion, we have perhaps found a way of doing this. As to where religion comes from, we have to go back in time as far back as in creation. There are but few people who have not heard the story of Adam and Eve and their relationship with their maker (God) This was the start of all the religions there are now in the world. They all have one thing in common, namely a god or deity as its head. Some call it Allah, some Buddha, some another name and with it comes the practice of worship via the different rites and ceremonies. The Christian faith has the same origin, namely through Adam and his son Abel, who no doubt had offsprings before he was slain by Cain, and so on we go to Enoch, to Noah, to Abraham, to the Israelites and from there to Rome and on to the reformation until we come to the King James Version of the Bible that has (in my opinion) the best translation from the Greek and other languages like Hebrew etc.

I have come to see that religion is a very personal thing and brings with it a belief in the things unseen as it is a total spiritual experience. There has to be an understanding that there is an end to all things, including our lives, and then what? We have to see that the promise of eternal life is not an idle one and that to achieve this is vital if we want to obtain it. The Bible is a teaching tool that is given to us by God, and he demands that we read it to gain an understanding of the workings of God in us through the Holy Spirit and through Christ who is the door through whom we may enter into that realm where all things are clear and are given an assurance of eternal life with no strings attached. I see that some words are more powerful than others as is in all subjects and I see how wonderful it is to be able to read and understand the meanings of whatever is written. Some people have the ability to say things so eloquently, and we have to admire them for that is a gift. I myself in my own humble way, try to convey to the readers of this chapter why religion came into the world.

Jesus states in the Bible that no one can come to the Father lest the Spirit draw him. He makes the Spirit the instrument that is needed to come to and to understand the meaning of all things. I realize that there are so many stumbling blocks which can be put in our way, as Satan will give nobody a free pass to eternal life if he can help it. Our spirit is constantly at war with the physical and it will be a fight to the end of our life and only those who will conquer the physical will enter into that realm which has been reserved for them from the beginning of time

13

WHERE ARE WE?

At times I wonder where we as a person or separate entity are in the grand scheme of things. What is our destiny, and what is our role? Are we the center piece of all what we see, including the universe? Is all what is around us just an illusion? I know this seems so silly to a lot of people reading this as we see things and experience things that explains reality to us, but was it reality? When we go back in time and understand creation, we come to see that the "big bang" set in motion that thing what we call "time." Before this moment, there was no time, only endlessness. It was the moment that our Creator decided that it was time to bring about all that we see now and bring into existence time and reality as we know it. All the universes were formed, as well as all the planets, and all the ingredients were there from which eventually life was formed in one form or another. It was called creation. I don't care if it started with a single cell. It was the Creator who called everything into being. All plant life, tree, grass, or bush came into existence in its several properties.

I have no argument with evolution as we know it or have been told. I believe that early animal life adapted to the environment that surrounded it. I realize that extreme changes in and on the earth caused some species to be completely wiped out, and we find the evidence all over the earth in the form of fossils unearthed by archaeologists. Nature has so many secrets that it would take a lifetime to unearth just some of them.

As far as we human beings are here for and what our purpose is, I explained in a earlier chapter. There is no doubt that a belief in something other than material things is necessary to get ready for the hereafter. We are all under the curse of death, and there is no escape from that.

When I was younger, I came to realize that I was not only one person but two in one. One was the physical body and the other the spiritual. The sooner we come to realize this, the better our chances are to understand that one is mortal and the other immortal. Now the question arises, "What about the immortal one?" Anyone who has taken the time to read the book given by our God and Father will begin to understand through the chapters written in there as to what has to take place before we pass over to that realm from where there is no returning from. There are so many books written by preachers of old, like Martin Luther, Calvin, Knox, as well as Swingley, who have tried to explain what has to happen to a human being to obtain eternal life. So now it is up to us to explore these teachings, and with the help of the Holy Spirit, come to the understanding of the place of God the Father, the Son, as well as the Holy Spirit in our lives, not only for the now but also for the hereafter.

14

ABOUT DEATH

When I thought about writing on this subject, I found it very disturbing. Who wants to talk about that, or in my case, write about it? We all know that death comes to all of us, and there is no getting away from it. In the Bible, there are only two or perhaps three cases in which a person was taken by God without dying first. The first one was Enoch and the other Elijah. There is another example of this in the story of Melchizedek who had no father and no mother according to some, was a high priest, and was a forerunner of the one to come—Jesus the Christ. But other than those, there is no mention of anyone who did not die a natural death.

We all know that death is an end of all living things—plants, animals, or humans. Even stars have a certain life expectancy before a supernova. And so it is that to everything there is an end. I look at death as a springboard into the unknown. It is an adventure as it were that takes us to where no one alive has ever been. It will be all new for us. We will be all knowing, and no one will have to explain to us what the reason is or was for having been born and living on this earth.

When we were born, it was almost as when a rock was thrown into the pond of life, which caused ever-widening circles that touched hundreds of individuals until finally the little waves touched the shore and we passed on, leaving only a memory to them who knew us.

15

WHAT IS HELL?

I wrote this with a capital *H* as it is a somewhat scary subject for most of us. The expression "Have been through hell and back" is quite common, especially for soldiers who have been through a fierce battle and did escape with their lives. A person having had a terrible experience because of a fire an accident or an illness can have had the feeling as to having been through hell. These expressions are but a small inkling as to what hell really is. As for myself, I have escaped death by the smallest of margins: three times I almost drowned and once when I was in a ship accident in Sweden when my head was almost crushed between the ship and the quay because of some foolishness. However, here I am still alive but only by the grace of God and nobody else.

I believe hell is a place where one cannot return from and where the anguish of loneliness is all consuming. We will see our lives as we lived it and the regrets of not having done everything possible to find the road to eternal life. The absence of God and all the people we knew in life will cause an unquenchable heartache to which there will be no end until there will be no more time.

God in his mercy will then do away with the evil one, who is and was the cause of all the evils done by mankind, and then all those who are in what we call hell will be thrown into the lake of fire and will be no more. This will be the second death, and the Age of Aquarius will begin with peace and goodwill towards all mankind.